ORGANIZING

FOR

NONVIOLENT

DIRECT ACTION

BY

CHARLES C. WALKER

About the Author:

Charles Coates "Charlie" Walker (1920-2004), a Philadelphia Quaker and American activist in the civil rights and peace movements, participated in the vast network of individuals and groups who supported Dr. Martin Luther King's nonviolent crusade for racial justice. In 1949 Walker helped introduce King, a student at Crozer Theological Seminary near Philadelphia, to nonviolence. Besides meeting with King twice and corresponding with him, Walker worked with King, A. Philip Randolph, James Farmer, James Lawson, Bayard Rustin, George Houser, baseball great Jackie Robinson and other key civil rights proponents. Walker organized marches and

Walker speaking at peace rally in Philadelphia, 1965
Photo by Theodore Hetzel

conferences, becoming a key trainer and writer of training materials. *Organizing for Nonviolent Direct Action* was the first handbook of its kind and was translated into seven languages. Walker helped organize the March on Washington in 1963 and its forerunners the Prayer Pilgrimage for Freedom and the Youth Marches for Integrated Schools in 1957 and 1958. He was on the training staff of the Mississippi Summer Project in 1964 and conducted the nonviolence training workshops for the Poor People's Campaign. In the 1970s and '80s Walker worked primarily in the Peace Movement. He co-founded World Peace Brigades, Peace Brigades International, the Gandhi-Woolman Institute and The Pennsylvania Committee to Abolish the Penalty of Death.

***

Charles Walker's daughter, Brenda Walker Beadenkopf decided to reprint *Organizing for Nonviolent Direct Action* after his death, as an important piece of his legacy. She hopes people will use these timeless principles in this new century as they were used in the 1960s, with constructive programs that exemplify "nonviolent attitudes in action."

***

Sincere thanks to Sara Palmer for the hours she spent converting the 1961 work into a digital file for today's media, and to William Beadenkopf for formatting and bringing the project together.

PREFACE

This handbook is designed to be of practical use to those groups on the American scene now adopting nonviolence in the struggle for peace and social justice.

It is not a definitive work covering every aspect of nonviolent direct action. Many items of importance have been omitted because any good organizer can cope with them. On the other hand, some detailed considerations have been included because they are sometimes overlooked or because they deal with problems peculiar to this mode of action.

While organizational matters are stressed I am assuming they must always be considered in context, must take second place to basic objectives and values, and must never be used as an excuse to push people around.

Organization and planning represent, in one sense, the "law" by which we must live unless we live more fully "in the spirit" which always seeks to break through the conventional and rehearsed response, and "bloweth where it listeth."

Charles C. Walker
1961

. . . .

ORGANIZING FOR NONVIOLENT DIRECT ACTION

Contents

SECTION I   GETTING STARTED

A. Select and clarify objectives, such as

   1. To dramatize an unjust situation
   2. To break an impasse in negotiations
   3. To protest an evil practice
   4. To mobilize public support
   5. To eradicate a specific injustice

B. Develop the will to resist

   1. Publish a continuous flow of information and analysis, calling for action now
   2. Analyze various alternatives open
      a. Inadequacy of present methods for dealing with the problem
      b. Possibility of explosion into violence and irrational or uncontrollable action
      c. Alternatives through nonviolent action
   3. Bring the skeptical or uncommitted face to face with the situation
   4. Expose the victims to an alternative situation (victims of segregation to an integrated situation or experience)
   5. Undertake pioneering action, e.g. use a segregated facility, remembering the "propaganda of the deed"

C. Consult with related organizations

   1. Consult with organizations with a similar or related purpose whose constituency may be affected by your action
   2. Consult with sympathetic or allied groups in the geographical area where the action will be taking place
   3. Try to secure names and addresses of people in the action area who may help; offer to turn over to cooperating groups the names and addresses of new people enlisted through the project
   4. Avoid handing out ready-made plans; seek advice and assistance at all levels of the developing situation
   5. If groups prove uncooperative, seek a policy of neutrality rather than of open criticism.

SECTION II   LAUNCHING A CONSTRUCTIVE PROGRAM

A. Definition: a program of attacking the roots of an evil or injustice, of helping the victims, of exemplifying nonviolent attitudes in action, and of developing what Vinoba Bhave calls "the self-reliant power of the people."

B. Values of a constructive program

1. All begin to work on the problem immediately
2. Helps participants to grow in their understanding of the problem and its implications
3. Provides a creative antidote to the negative feelings of apathy and resentment
4. Develops the specific virtues needed for nonviolent resistance: self-discipline, persistence, patience, self-reliance, respect for all persons, endurance of hardships, living cheerfully under corporate discipline, serving human need, initiative, etc.
5. Builds popular support
6. Exemplifies the attitude of selfless service to the community, thus building confidence in the movement and its integrity

C. Examples of constructive work in the USA that can be especially helpful in preparation for nonviolent action

1. Work camps, weekend or summer
2. Cooperatives
3. Assistance to victims of injustice
4. Some aspects of do-it-yourself work
5. Work in gardens or orchards
6. Works of mercy and relief of suffering
7. Work in community service agencies

D. A complement to direct action

1. There is no "lull" in the movement when direct action campaigns are suspended
2. Constructive work, especially that which involves physical work, is emotionally helpful after a period of high tension

NOTE: Read Edmond Taylor RICHER BY ASIA pp. 404-418, Douglas Steere WORK AND CONTEMPLATION, chapters 6-7 in Karl Menninger LOVE AGAINST HATE, and Daniel Bell WORK AND ITS DISCONTENTS.

SECTION III   LEARNING THE METHOD

A. Seven steps to nonviolent direct action

    1. Investigation...find out

        a. Facts and attitudes regarding grievances

        b. Underlying forces related to the issue: social, political, economic, etc..

        c. The community power structure

        d. Role of the press, police and political leaders

        e. Attitude of key community groups

        f. The legal situation

        g. Responsibility for policy-making

        h. Sources of rumors

        i. Actual facts of recurring stories of key incidents

        j. Next steps that community agencies and/or leaders are prepared to take

    2. Negotiation

        a. On basis of findings, seek a policy change

        b. Be sure you are dealing with those able to change or influence policy

        c. Use all negotiating agencies available in the community

        d. Keep detailed records of all negotiations

        e. Study Elmore Jackson MEETING OF MINDS

    3. Mobilization of public opinion

        a. Use mass media: radio, TV, newspapers; seek editorials, news and feature stories, photos, interviews

        b. Use speakers, public meetings, home meetings, film showings, dramatizations

        c. Urge public speeches, sermons

        d. Publish special bulletins, flyers, pamphlets, reprints of articles and speeches

        e. Take public opinion polls, or community audits and surveys

        f. Seek public statements of key people, individually or corporately

        g. Encourage resolutions of support and publicize them

        h. Circulate petitions

        i. Conduct demonstrations, rallies

        j. Organize deputations and delegations

        k. Appeal to special groups: church, labor, farm,

education, youth, professional, civic, business, political, ethnic
   1. Constantly carry on conversations with community leaders
4. Extraordinary appeals
   a. Mayor (he often has great, even decisive, influence with political, business or community leaders, as well as with the police or those in higher levels of state or national government)
   b. Governor
   c. Attorney General, state or national
   d. President or Vice-President of the US
   e. Note: offer to agree to arbitration or mediation services of a community or government agency, or by a special citizens committee
5. Sacrificial action
   a. Day of fasting and prayer
   b. Pilgrimage to make an appeal
   c. Offer an important concession if it does not violate principle or basic objective
   d. Renounce special honors or awards given by those practicing the injustice (but think this through very carefully)
6. Ultimatum
   a. List specific grievances, past attempts to negotiate, concessions offered and reactions to them
   b. Since all prior actions have not brought results or have led only to delays or even retaliation, set a deadline for action on minimum demands
   c. Put it in writing to the policy makers
   d. Inform others who may be affected
7. Direct action (See C "Forms of nonviolent direct...")
   a. Embark on direct action only as a last resort when all attempts at persuasion fail, when waiting appears to worsen matters and when the only alternative is continuance of an intolerable situation

B. Three admonitions

   1. Keep up negotiations all along the way
      a. Negotiation will be needed some time anyway
      b. Opponents can see each other as persons and not just obstacles or heartless pursuers of advantage

   c. Each side can counteract false rumors or
    inaccurate statements about its position
   d. Avoid haggling or "horse-trading"
  2. Keep your constituency informed every step of the
   way
   a. Publish articles and stories in related news
    outlets, and in the press
   b. Hold periodic meetings
   c. Note: an appeal to direct action can be made
    successfully only when the potential
    participants as well as the leaders are
    convinced no other honorable way can be taken—
    for the cost of the struggle may be high and
    the length considerable
  3. Cooperate with your opponent when on honorable terms,
   e.g. joining in support of a community enterprise

C. Forms of nonviolent direct action

  1. Vigil at a site symbolizing the problem
  2. Picketing
  3. Fasting or hunger strike
  4. Noncooperation, e.g. farmers refusing to buy
   neighbor's farm sold in foreclosure
  5. Boycott
  6. Work stoppage for a brief period
  7. Strike
  8. Reverse strike, e.g. Dolci leading unemployed to
   work building road when forbidden
  9. Intervention, e.g. going into forbidden area and
   refusing to leave
  10. Civil disobedience
  11. Migration
  12. Demonstrations—rallies, marches, protests (Note:
   since opponents may attack these demonstrations and
   seek to precipitate disorder and violence, these may
   be considered marginal forms of direct action)

D. An amalgam of power and persuasion

  1. Nonviolent direct action combines the social power of
   noncooperation with the moral power of voluntary
   suffering for others
  2. Even the action can be seen as a form of persuasion;
   the aim is to change the will of the adversary
  3. Read Gene Sharp "A Typology Of Nonviolence" in THE
   JOURNAL OF CONFLICT RESOLUTION March 1959

SECTION IV   TRAINING

A. Study the theory and practice of nonviolence

1. THE POWER OF NONVIOLENCE by Richard Gregg,
   Fellowship Publications, 2nd revised edition
2. CIVIL DISOBEDIENCE by Henry D. Thoreau. In Mentor
   edition with Walden
3. A PERSPECTIVE ON NONVIOLENCE prepared by the Friends
   Peace Committee
4. SPEAK TRUTH TO POWER prepared by the American
   Friends Service Committee
5. NONVIOLENCE IN AN AGGRESSIVE WORLD by A. J. Muste.
   Check public library
6. NEITHER VICTIMS NOR EXECUTIONERS by Albert Camus. A
   reprint from LIBERATION Feb. 1960
7. ESSAYS ON NONVIOLENT DIRECT ACTION by Bradford Lyttle,
   published by the author
8. WAR WITHOUT VIOLENCE by K. Shridharani. Hard to
   find; is in Swarthmore Peace Collection

B. Study nonviolent campaigns in detail

1. PASSIVE RESISTANCE IN SOUTH AFRICA by Leo Kuper.
   Yale University Press (paper)
2. STRIDE TOWARD FREEDOM by Martin Luther King.
   Ballantine Books
3. GANDHI by Louis Fischer. Mentor
4. TYRANNY COULD NOT QUELL THEM by Gene Sharp. Peace
   News reprint 1959
5. THE CONQUEST OF VIOLENCE by Joan Bondurant.
   Princeton University Press
6. THE VOYAGE OF THE GOLDEN RULE by Albert Bigelow.
   Doubleday
7. "Settling a Sit-In" By Wallace Westfeldt, in MOTIVE
   Magazine (Methodist) October 1960
8. CHRISTIANS IN THE ARENA by Allan A. Hunter.
   Fellowship Publications
9. "Stages of Nonviolence" by Andre Trocme in FELLOWSHIP
   Magazine, October 1953
10. WHEN NEGROES MARCH by Herbert Garfinkel. Free Press

C. Observe direct action in operation when possible

D. Conduct street meetings (excellent small scale models of
   larger problems to face)

E. Conduct a regularly meeting study group, using this handbook as a study guide

F. Conduct a workshop on nonviolence

    1. Present basic outline of theory and practice
    2. Study photographs, slides or films of violent situations
    3. Show films of demonstrations or other actions
        a. "Voices of Hiroshima" (Japan demonstrat.)
        b. "The Language of Faces" (Quaker, Vigil)
        c. "Deadly The Harvest" (Britain, Aldermaston)
           Note: write AFSC, 1501 Cherry St., Phila, PA 19102
    4. Plan and hold a street meeting
    5. Use role playing (see handbook published by Adult Education Ass'n, 743 N. Wabash Ave., Chicago 11, Ill; Leadership Pamphlet #6)[*]

G. Examine personal comportment

    1. Cleanliness of clothes and person
    2. Neatness in personal surroundings
    3. Punctuality
    4. Cheerfulness in the daily round
    5. Special notes
        a. The group will be accused of being dirty, disorderly, undependable, neurotic, etc. Cultivation of orderly habits enhances self respect and public respect.
        b. To avoid pride or priggishness regarding such discipline, temper these virtues with humor.
        c. Study Gregg (A-1) Chapters 10-11

H. Learn the practice of regular meditation (there is a vast literature on this subject; for a beginning see Thomas Kelly REALITY OF THE SPIRITUAL WORLD (Pendle Hill), Douglas Steere WORK AND CONTEMPLATION (American Friends Service Committee); for further study see Thomas Powers FIRST QUESTIONS IN THE LIFE OF THE SPIRIT (Harper), Richard Gregg THE SELF BEYOND YOURSELF (Lippincott) chapters 17-18)

---

[*] Currently, American Association for Adult and Continuing Education (AAACE). AEA archives are stored at: Special Collections Research Center, Syracuse University Libraries, 222 Waverly Avenue, Syracuse, NY 13244-2010

I. Use group singing, dancing, recounting of heroic achievement especially of courageous and creative action, group meditation, shared meals

J. Habits and attitudes developed in carrying on constructive work will be helpful in developing confidence in the kinds of forces upon which nonviolence relies.

SECTION V   PLANNING FOR DIRECT ACTION

A. Select appropriate form of direct action

  1. The apt form should grow organically out of the logic of the situation and the sentiments of those involved

  2. The form chosen should be actually or potentially within the understanding and capability of those involved

  3. Do not give undue weight to considerations of publicity (though one must be circumspect, see later) but rather be sure the action to be taken truly and aptly expresses the deepest truths and feelings those undertaking it wish to communicate

B. Select a point of concentration, e.g. a physical site, a law, a public facility

C. Establish the organizational structure

  1. Select form, such as

    a. Existing group

    b. Ad hoc organization, of groups or of individuals or a combination

    c. A coordinated effort

  2. Work out organizational relationships with friendly and allied groups

  3. Develop clear lines of authority and of responsibility

  4. Provide a clear procedure for making decisions

  5. Appoint committees and/or coordinators

    a. Project committee, the over-all group

    b. Administrative committee

    c. Project director

    d. Coordinators or committees, such as

      (1) Community relations

      (2) Action leadership

      (3) Publicity

        (4) Office management

        (5) Transportation

        (6) Literature production

        (7) Housing

        (8) Food

        (9) Finances (See Section VI-C)

        (10) Volunteers

        (11) Communications (in large actions)

D. Develop a time-table

1. Be mindful of the symbolism that can be invoked at the inauguration of the project or on special occasions or at the end
2. Schedule preliminary activities—rallies, vigils, training sessions—and announce them well in advance
3. Do not announce the time-table or events before full consultation with groups involved, a walk through specified towns for example
4. Keep to the time-table; participants must work out personal arrangements, action is less likely to get bogged down in frustrating delays, and a sense of movement is imparted to the whole enterprise

E. Mobilize special resources needed, such as

1. Training specialists
2. Legal counsel
3. Financial advisers (draw up rough budget)
4. Allies in the community
5. Allies outside the community
6. Organizational specialists
7. Publicity specialists

SECTION VI   PREPARING FOR DIRECT ACTION

A. Open headquarters

1. Select location carefully for its convenience and possible symbolism
2. May be a store front, church basement, rented building, tent, trailer
3. Keep quarters neat and clean
4. Post displays, notices, banners, enlarged photographs, news stories, cartoons
5. Announce opening
6. Might hold a press conference at the opening

B. Send formal advance notices of the impending action

    1. Letters to appropriate officials
    2. Possible follow-up visits
    3. Letters to others directly affected
    4. Ads in the papers, radio and TV talks

C. Finances

    1. Open special bank account if needed
    2. Be clear on tax-exemption problems
    3. Set up a simple system of bookkeeping (the treasurer may be arrested)
    4. Exercise fanatical care and probity in financial matters (in addition to the usual reasons, there may be charges of misuse of funds or official investigations)
    5. Have periodic audits of accounts
    6. Draw up a budget
    7. Seek out sources of income
        a. mailings to selected lists
        b. collections at rallies and mass meetings
        c. contributions from constituency
        d. mutual aid funds
        e. special "defense" funds
        f. "gifts in kind"
        g. pledges payable at stated times

D. Arrange for meeting places

    1. Large halls or churches or auditorium for mass meetings or rallies
    2. Meeting rooms for committees, consultations
    3. Action assembly points
    4. Facilities for feeding large crowds if needed

E. Lay in supplies

    1. First-rate typewriter for cutting stencils
    2. Additional typewriters
    3. Dependable mimeograph machine and supplies
    4. Tools and equipment
    5. Emergency cots and sleeping bags
    6. Letterhead, postage, stationery
    7. Poster materials
    8. Furniture, chairs, filing cabinet
    9. Cars arranged for

F. Compile information on nearby services

G. Establish mailing address

H. Develop system of communications

1. Phones, preferably more than one line
2. Loudspeakers or walkie-talkies for movement of large groups (in the thousands)
3. Cars for special messengers
4. Daily bulletins in large actions that last more than a day or so
5. If arrests are likely, observers should be chosen who will not court arrest but will be charged with transmitting information on the action to headquarters or action direction point
6. All important messages should be written down: to whom, from whom, from where, time

I. Prepare instructions

1. Mimeograph details of group movements to be distributed to each participant
2. Mimeograph copies of the corporate discipline (See Section VIII)
3. Prepare precise and full instructions for each group leader and coordinator
4. Prepare advance information or questions to be sent to participants prior to arrival

J. Register participants in advance when possible

1. To send information as it develops
2. To find out what skills the participants will have
3. To get a "sounding" on how the project seems to be catching on, what problems it is raising, what image is emerging

K. Prepare posters, leaflets and other materials

1. Make all signs neat and attractive
2. Paint key signs in black letters, big enough and thick enough to photograph well
3. Legends on signs should be short and clear; avoid name-calling; repeat main slogans; committee approve all signs prior to use

4. When high tension may result, do not affix posters to sticks, which may injure someone if attacked and the group will be blamed (!) but tie two posters together over shoulders for "sandwich sign" effect
5. Select leaflets already in print if appropriate, or assign committee to prepare them
6. Write clear leaflets, long enough to carry message, succinct enough to encourage its immediate reading
7. Be clear on the purpose of the leaflet, and what you propose the recipient does about it
8. Prepare leaflets and posters in plenty of time-- delays do occur

SECTION VII   EXPLORING THE LEGAL SITUATION

A. Check property lines, public and private

B. Check relevant local ordinances

1. Assembly, e.g. in some states or towns interracial assembly is illegal
2. Leaflet distribution (cannot be forbidden except when it constitutes a traffic hazard or a "public nuisance")
3. Permits for use of public buildings
4. Permits for parades or processions
5. Street meeting problems (permits cannot be required legally but this is not always realized by authorities; give prior notice to police department)

C. Know where legal help can be secured

1. Lawyer
2. Nearby magistrate, for certain legal recourses
3. Bondsman or source of bail money

SECTION VIII   WORKING OUT A CORPORATE DISCIPLINE

A. Three functions of a corporate discipline

1. "A discipline is like a tool. Tools, whether tangible or intangible, make it possible for ordinary men to do what was formerly possible only to men of very unusual skill, strength or intellect." (Gregg)
2. It helps prevent actions or reactions which bring disunity or disorder, or which work against the objectives of the action

      3. It provides a way by which a group of people can do corporately what they wish to do

B. Participation should be made conditional upon acceptance of the discipline--no exceptions should be permitted

C. Its provisions should be approved by the Project Committee

D. Suggested discipline in simplified form

      1. We will endeavor to maintain an attitude of good will at all times, especially in face of provocation or unsettling conditions

      2. If violence occurs against us, we will not retaliate but will strive to practice forgiveness and forbearance

      3. We agree to the provision that one person be in charge of specific actions and agree to abide by the decisions of the person in charge, even if at the time we do not fully agree with or understand the decision

      4. If in good conscience we cannot comply with this decision, we will not take contrary action but will withdraw from that phase of the action, trusting there will not be a feeling of censure or broken fellowship by any parties to the decision

      5. In the event of arrest, we will submit to the arresting process with promptness and with composure

      6. We shall endeavor to be punctual in our appointments, and to carry out responsibly those tasks for which we have volunteered or to which we have been assigned

      7. While participating in the project, we will abide by the policy decisions of the Project Committee

      8. We will present our considered views with due regard for the view of others, yet seek to act with one accord

E. Adherence to discipline depends on many factors, especially loyalty, courage and dedicated purpose

SECTION IX   DEVELOPING A PUBLICITY CAMPAIGN

A. Clarify purposes

1. To get your story before the public
2. To try to insure that your views and statements will be reported accurately and in your words
3. To correct false impressions, rumors, stories
4. To augment the outreach of the project
5. To reach unknown sympathizers

B. Draw up a prospectus and time-table

C. Prepare...

1. Background information sheet
2. Brief biographical sketches of well-known leaders and participants, as well as those with special "human interest"
3. Suggestions on how to prepare and issue a news release, when several local groups are involved
4. Model for a release to their local paper by participants

D. Issue news releases, for example to

1. Metropolitan dailies in the nation
2. Wire services: AP and UPI
3. Special press services: Religious News Service, labor press, etc.
4. Neighborhood papers in the area
5. Foreign language press when relevant
6. News departments of both TV and radio
7. Editorial writers of key papers
8. Commentators: TV, radio, columnists
9. Editors of newsletters

E. Utilize radio and television

1. Offer advance interviews
2. Prepare for coverage of newsworthy events and personalities
3. Consider purchasing special broadcast time periodically; this reaches important constituencies on all sides of the issue
4. Tape record important speeches for broadcast

F. Visit key people

    1. Editors
    2. Radio and TV news directors
    3. Special reporters

G. Write letters to the editor

    1. From project officials periodically
    2. From participants
    3. From supporters

H. Suggestions for "on the action scene"

    1. Assign one person to handle all press tasks; he may assign individuals to carry out special tasks at the time
    2. Beware of "off-the-record" remarks
    3. Check where reporters and photographers are from, for later followup work
    4. Be clear on who is authorized to speak for the project

I. General suggestions

    1. Don't let publicity factors distort the project, especially at its opening
    2. Keep feeding information out regularly
    3. Ask supporters to act as a "clipping service" marking date and paper on clippings
    4. Don't be unduly eager to secure publicity; the task is to inform, not to see a name or picture on the paper, or to exaggerate the project's significance or accomplishments
    5. Be zealously careful to be accurate regarding quotations; check and double-check
    6. Keep detailed records of publicity releases and summaries; periodically post or publish press summaries
    7. Reprint important stories or appropriate photos as a leaflet for local distribution; make up a montage of photos and clippings
    8. Be mindful of ways that local and national (or regional) stories support each other, and how each adds impetus to a developing story
    9. Study handbook on standard publicity practice

SECTION X   ASSEMBLING THE PARTICIPANTS

A. Register participants

1. To locate in emergency
2. To compile information for publicity purposes
3. To record names, addresses and skills to assist committees in their planning
4. To build mailing list for later bulletins, finance appeals, action suggestions
   Note: have adequate number of registrars; delay in registration is a frequent cause of confusion and schedules gone awry

B. Greet individuals warmly; make them feel a part of the enterprise right from the start

C. Hold a keynote meeting

1. See Section IV-I on building group unity
2. Reiterate major objectives and plan of action
3. Read supporting statements and resolutions
4. Present informative and inspirational talks
5. Distribute relevant literature
6. Outline procedures and instructions: role playing or demonstration may be appropriate
7. Deal with questions and problems
8. "Set the tone" for the whole undertaking

D. In protracted efforts, periodic convocations will be needed to

1. Bring new participants into a sense of unity
2. Explain new or revised procedures
3. Report on new developments, proposals
4. Take action on policy matters

E. Two suggestions

1. Choose meeting chairmen carefully; he should be clear on meeting objectives; will be a major factor in communicating confidence in the cause and its leadership; avoid temptation to choose "big name" without weighing sufficiently factors listed above
2. Differentiate carefully between matters to be brought to general meetings and those better left to the administrative committee

SECTION XI   INITIATING THE ACTION

A. Select initiators carefully

    1. In actions where violence or disorder may result (not from initiating group but from adversaries, bystanders or police) choose a small number of the best disciplined and most dependable persons

    2. Do not choose initiators just because they volunteer but because they meet the qualifications; name a committee to make selections

    3. Provide for replacements or next contingent

    4. Choose or appoint a spokesman

B. Gather at assembly point

    1. Schedule adequate time for group movements, especially of large crowds; otherwise the schedule cannot be kept or leaders tend to use "herding" techniques

    2. Distribute materials, such as signs, leaflets, insignia (arm bands, buttons, badges)

    3. Give instructions clearly; reiterate rather than assume too much

C. Start the action

    1. From assembly point go to action site as instructed

    2. Take greatest pains to avoid confusion and to carry out the initial action with order and dignity

    3. Group leaders set the example and others will quickly "pick up the tone"

    4. Participants refer questioners, police or press to action coordinator or spokesman as directed; he will either handle the problem or assign someone to do it

    5. Stand or walk or sit erectly and composedly: do not slouch, fidget, call out, laugh loudly, indulge in antics or use profanity; in some situations, smoking may be ruled out

    6. Follow instructions of group leaders promptly and cheerfully

    7. Do not leave assigned place without personal notification to group leader

8. Refrain from taking photos while in assigned place; check with group leader on time and propriety of it

D. Distributing leaflets (if involved in the action)

1. Assign two people to each location unless obviously unnecessary
2. Be sure an adequate supply of leaflets is provided periodically to the leafleteers
3. Instruct leafleteers on how to answer very briefly when asked "What is this all about" or "Who's doing this"
4. Give careful thought on how to give a quick identification of the group
5. Leafleteers pick up all discarded leaflets (to avoid legal charge of "littering")
6. If in a street, sidewalk, or public area, avoid interfering with pedestrian or vehicular traffic; do not give leaflets to passing cars (in exceptional cases it may be better to give a leaflet to one in a car who is requesting it if your hesitation threatens to cause a traffic jam)
7. In rainy weather, keep leaflets in plastic bag

E. Suggestions on conducting a silent vigil

1. Stand comfortably erect but not rigidly
2. Keep the silence as absolute as possible; only rarely can a comment be so important or world-shaking that it cannot be deferred
3. Walk in some orderly pattern about every half-hour, for a few minutes, more frequently if the weather is cold; this should not be considered a "break" in the vigil
4. Change shifts about every two hours
5. Use signs very sparingly
6. Concentrate on the QUALITY of the vigil; here numbers are not decisive, faithfulness is

F. Notes to leaders

1. Avoid unnecessary scurrying about
2. Give instructions in clear and authoritative voice but avoid peremptory orders and domineering approach
3. Example of leadership will be felt throughout

SECTION XII   FACING RETALIATION

A. Provocation

1. A major objective of the opponent may be to provoke the group into
   a. Intemperate statements
   b. Accusations that are overstated or imprecise and cannot be proved
   c. Name-calling in retaliation
   d. Excited or undignified behavior
   e. Confusion and disorder
   f. Mutual recrimination among the leaders
   g. Defections from the ranks
   h. Violence
2. Avoid trying, in dealing with provocative actions, to be "too clever" and "playing games" but keep one's inner composure; keep cool under fire; in face of ridicule, abuse or trickery, remain friendly and honorable toward your tormentor
3. Be more than restrained, be creative, be open to the inspired initiative; in the Quaker phrase "speak to that of God in every man"

B. Violence

1. Perfect and control the instruments by which to control, contain or prevent the violence
   a. Commitment to nonviolence
   b. Adherence to corporate discipline
   c. Loyalty of participants to each other
   d. The "order of the action" (not breaking ranks)
2. Participants act only on instructions from group leader—do not intervene except to help an injured person—remember that those who joined this action have been prepared to accept violence if it comes-- yet still be mindful of the possibility of the creative response if it comes to you
3. Pray for the victim and the attacker
4. If the blow is not too severe or disabling, the person attacked may try to take the initiative; for example, in the calmest voice he can muster, he may say: "Sir, may I ask you a question?" (Study Allan Hunter COURAGE IN BOTH HANDS, Fellowship Publications)
5. Group leader supervise removal of injured persons,

giving first aid if necessary or providing for
medical attention

6. Sometimes a group may spontaneously start singing a
hymn or repeating a prayer together

7. Do not appeal to the police for aid

8. Note carefully the attitude of onlookers, for their
attitude may be crucial, not only in determining
the physical outcome of the incident but
interpreting it and its effects to the public later

9. Remember sometimes a man doesn't come to his senses
until he sees himself committing violence to
perpetuate his privileged position or his evil or
unjust practice

C. Arrest and imprisonment

1. With rare exceptions, do not resist the arresting
process and make it clear in advance that this is
your intention

2. Think through whether to pay fines if levied or
accept bail if stipulated

3. Seek advice and think through how to plead in
hearings or trials
   a. Guilty
   b. Not guilty
   c. Nolle contendere

4. Consider whether to accept or waive a lawyer's
services at the hearing or trial; a lawyer who does
not share your nonviolent approach may precipitate
an unfortunate "emotional climate" in the courtroom

5. If imprisoned, comply with prison routines and
discipline cheerfully, except in cases of outrageous
indignities or orders to commit an act that violates
conscience

6. Read Alfred Hassler DIARY OF A SELFMADE CONVICT for
authentic picture of prison life, Fellowship
Publications

7. Think through carefully the implications of accepting
conditions of probation or parole if offered

8. Representatives of the group should visit the
families of those imprisoned, helping in hardship
cases

9. Do not deliberately seek arrest or imprisonment but
if it comes as a result of dedicated action, accept
it not as a grim necessity but as an honorable
service for the cause for which you are striving

10. Read IF YOU ARE ARRESTED, a leaflet published by the American Civil Liberties Union, 150 Fifth Avenue, New York 10, N.Y.

D. Reprisals

1. May include
   a. Beating, chain-whipping
   b. Shooting into houses or gatherings
   c. Mutilation or torture
   d. Bombings of homes, headquarters, meetings
   e. Threats of many kinds
   f. Harassment, even of children
   g. Nasty or threatening phone calls
   h. Lynching
   i. Stoning
   j. Taking of hostages, kidnapping
   k. Confiscation of property
   l. Boycott, counter-boycott
   m. Lockout
   n. Dismissal from job or position
   o. Legal suits
   p. Banning of organizations, assemblies
   q. Mass arrests
   Note: all these have happened in the South recently in the United States; many subtler reprisals have also been applied

2. May be directed against
   a. Leaders
   b. Participants and/or their relatives, friends
   c. Supporters or sympathizers
   d. Even innocent bystanders
3. May constitute the most severe test of group unity and perseverance
4. Urge responsible community leaders to ACT against violence and lawlessness (acting is not the same as deploring it)
5. Call for an inquiry by a government official, agency or civic committee
6. Render every possible and spiritual assistance to the victims, especially to those who did not choose to be involved

7. Remember constantly that these vicious actions result from the poisons that have been produced by long-inflicted injustices and entrenched evils, that counter-violence or counter-reprisals will only spread these poisons (even to one's own group), that they can be removed only by the voluntary and redemptive suffering of those who accept the responsibility to act decisively against these evils

SECTION XIII   NURTURING THE MOVEMENT

A. Develop new symbols

1. Heroic actions and those who performed them
2. Victims of retaliation
3. Those imprisoned
4. Anniversaries of outstanding events
5. Special observances
6. Salutations
7. Special buttons, badges, garments, arm bands

B. Keep up efforts at persuasion

1. Keep major objectives before the public
2. Seek support from the uncommitted or uncertain
3. Especially seek to persuade one's adversaries, e.g. appeal to those who have committed violence to refuse to be a party to such indignities any longer and join the movement
4. Keep constituency informed regularly, especially of progress toward the objective, supporting actions, contributions made by participants, etc.
5. Seek to widen the constituency of supporters and participants

C. Encourage and organize supporting actions

1. Statements from prominent individuals
2. Resolutions from sympathetic groups
3. Parallel local actions
4. Supporting demonstrations or rallies
5. Visits or letters to officials
6. Mutual aid groups

D. Keep the initiative

1. Respond creatively to acts of retaliation,

       slander or reprisals

2. Experiment with new approaches when an impasse seems to be developing
3. Develop new proposals and offers for negotiation
4. Keep "digging deeper into the problem" or it will prove to be increasingly difficult even to "hold the line"

Note: many problems can be dealt with best by putting them in the context of a new initiative taken by the group

E. Deal patiently and fairly with dissidents

1. Do not use undemocratic methods in face of any challenge to leadership, discipline or objectives
2. Recognize in grievances and protests, even from those temperamentally so inclined, symptoms revealing the state of underlying relationships; consider not only the "facts" of the grievance or provocation but the emotions and feelings it reflects
3. Expose agents provocateurs but avoid righteous anger and retaliation; seek to win them to the movement (or re-win them, for usually they are disaffected supporters whom the opponents find it possible to use)
4. Try to handle the situations that arise without public censure; by trying to work out the problems quietly and personally, the dissidents may find it easier to change their views and actions, and the movement will be spared much unpleasantness
5. Special note of relations with Communists or other political or organizational opportunists—the record shows that Communists operate both through the usual machinery of a political party and political persuasion, as well as through secretive and unscrupulous maneuvering; if Communists, known or believed to be such, join in an action as individuals and not in significant numbers, the leaders of the action will wish to satisfy themselves on the motivations and objectives of these participants, and under some circumstances may ask them to leave; none such should be permitted in the organizational structure;

but on the other hand, attempts to subvert or deflect the group from its central objectives or its commitment to nonviolence should be resisted quickly, decisively and democratically. Communists have no monopoly on unscrupulous tactics, it should be noted. Indiscriminate charges of Communism, or indiscriminate charges of "red-baiting" are unworthy of those dedicated to humane and democratic values. For background on how Communist groups operate, read Rossi A COMMUNIST PARTY IN ACTION (Yale), Selznick THE ORGANIZATIONAL WEAPON (Free Press) or Crossman (Ed.) THE GOD THAT FAILED (Bantam).

F. Carry on continuous training, education and instruction of the participants in the ranks

1. All need reinforcement of basic ideas, values
2. New leadership is constantly required, both in the normal course of events and especially when one group of leaders has been arrested or injured or isolated (banned)
3. Study and discussion of both theory and practice of nonviolence should be encouraged and not dismissed as ivory-tower escapism or mere speculation (any more than those enamored of theory should disdain the "merely practical")
4. Note comment of military expert: "It must be accepted as a principle that training carries on into the battle zone until the end of combat and that there is no release from it, even for the best of troops." (Marshall MEN AGAINST FIRE, Apollo Editions, p. 107)

G. Use volunteers extensively and significantly

1. In spite of its difficulty and complexity, this should be done in order to
   a. Spread the work load
   b. Enhance unity and morale
   c. Discover and develop new leadership
   d. Prevent concentration of power in the hands of an elite leadership
   e. Prepare the way for democratic participation in the new order of society the movement is seeking to bring into being

2. Volunteers should be provided with the opportunity for significant responsibility, decision-making and initiative; they should not be confined to routine tasks alone

3. A movement in which participants are deeply, regularly and individually involved in its workings is the most antidote to many ills, as for example
   a. False charges of manipulation by a few power-hungry leaders
   b. Feelings of vainglory by a few outstanding leaders
   c. Agents provocateurs and disrupters
   d. Inherent tendencies to bureaucracy
   e. Defeatism in difficult times

H. Morale

1. Morale is not a separate and autonomous category apart from the foregoing considerations in this section; it represents the totality of response the participants make; it is the thinking and feeling of the group

2. Morale will be high if the experience of the participants offers them the opportunity to live creatively, surmount ordeals, serve as a channel of constructive energies, and work loyally with their fellows who are with them dedicated to common values and purposes

3. "True discipline is the product of morale." (Marshall, op. cit., p. 159)

4. Participants need to feel and believe that they are not just cogs in the machine or a name on a filing card, but that they belong to a group which is concerned about them as persons, and about their welfare

5. Morale will not necessarily grow through a verbal commitment to a cause or group, or through an expressed determination to "do my share of the work," or through estimates of the success of this action or that, but rather will be grounded in the concrete activities of everyday life.

I. The group should exemplify, in many and various ways, nonviolence as the hallmark of its character.

SECTION XIV   LEADERSHIP

A. The qualities needed are those generally required for successful leadership in group enterprises; one major difference can be noted in leadership for nonviolent actions: the authoritarian structure or tradition has no place, at least on the American scene.

B. Teamwork needs to be developed among the leaders prior to the action, and if possible during the training period beforehand.

C. The Coordinator should not consider himself "over" the whole operation but as one with a significant function: coordination. Others might consider him "first among equals" in his functional role.

D. Decisions, to be sound, must be based on accurate information, much of which will be brought into the picture by the leadership; reports should be precise, distinguishing between judgment and fact, presenting the ungarnished story; the cumulative effect of inaccurate information is a substantial obstacle to effective functioning.

E. A cardinal requirement of leadership is the ability to think clearly when faced with unexpected contingencies or opportunities. "Improvisation is of the essence of initiative...just as initiative is the outward showing of the power of decision." (Marshall, op. cit., p. 117)

F. Prior to the action, the top leadership should maintain a balance between shaping up the project and perfecting the interior workings of the group; when the action begins, they must rely on those with assigned responsibilities to carry out their tasks ("trouble-shooting" will of course be necessary) and concentrate their thought and energies on the "horizon" of the action.

G. The finest quality good leaders possess is the blending of undeviating and dedicated commitment with flexibility in tactics and sensitivity to human feelings. Such leaders soon earn the loyalty of their fellow workers in good measure.

SECTION XV   FACING PROTRACTED STRUGGLE

A. Gandhi listed five typical responses to a nonviolent campaign: indifference, ridicule, abuse, repression, and respect; it may take sustained action or many campaigns to win the ultimate objective.

B. The constructive program takes on added significance in a protracted conflict; prolonged resistance can wear down an opponent but the objective is not his defeat but his conversion; the composite effect of sustained and heroic resistance through nonviolence, and of the positive achievements through work and service, can win the uncommitted (whose influence may be decisive).

C. There may be difference of view whether to broaden the objectives of the action or movement, or on the other hand to concentrate on one key objective; both strategies have merit; usually a decision on this matter is not automatically deduced from a principle but is based on a judgment or "sense of the situation."

D. What is being sought is not a victory or defeat in a narrow personal or organizational sense, but a transformation of relationships: within a social structure or between individuals and groups who function in it, or in a new social order; the victory will be for justice and human decency; segregation may lose but segregationists may win their freedom--from enslavement to a "house upon sand." This transformation of relationships must be kept central in the whole enterprise from start to finish, in attitudes toward those both inside and outside the group undertaking the action.

E. Protracted struggle may be necessary, for ancient wrongs are not quickly righted nor do exploiters readily yield the fruits of their exploitation; organization will be required, but it tends to perpetuate itself and therefore to perpetuate the cleavages between contending groups; the practitioners of nonviolence should seek to transcend the outward struggle and bring all parties into a more creative relationship.

F. "(The power of Truth) is a force vaster than weapons or prisons, more compelling than fame or fear or success or money, more penetrating than any of the notions whereby men try to enlarge their egos or to gain face in the outward conduct of their lives. It conquers oppression, settles fear, shakes the hearts of the strong, strengthens the muscles of the weak." (Herrymon Maurer THE POWER OF TRUTH)

. . . .

SUGGESTIONS FOR FURTHER READING

THE FUNCTIONS OF SOCIAL CONFLICT by Lewis Coser. Free Press, 1956.

SATYAGRAHA IN SOUTH AFRICA by M. K. Gandhi. Academic Reprints (Stanford, Calif.), 1954.

A TIME TO SPEAK by Michael Scott. Doubleday, 1958. Experiences in African movements.

THE CRISIS OF AMERICAN LABOR by Sidney Lens. Sagamore, 1959.

CRUSADER WITHOUT VIOLENCE by L. D. Reddick. Harper, 1959. About the Montgomery Bus Protest.

BIBLIOGRAPHY ON WAR, PACIFISM, NONVIOLENCE, AND RELATED STUDIES, Fellowship Publications, Nyack, N.Y., 1959.

. . . .

April 1961

www.ingramcontent.com/pod-product-compliance
Lightning Source LLC
Chambersburg PA
CBHW050527290526
45786CB00007B/2724